Wild Flock

Wild Flock

Seeing God's Love and Splendor in Everyday Life

Susie Grade

ELM HILL

A Division of
HarperCollins Christian Publishing

www.elmhillbooks.com

Wild Flock
Seeing God's Love and Splendor in Everyday Life

Published in Nashville, Tennessee, by Elm Hill, an imprint of Thomas Nelson. Elm Hill and Thomas Nelson are registered trademarks of HarperCollins Christian Publishing, Inc.

Elm Hill titles may be purchased in bulk for educational, business, fund-raising, or sales promotional use. For information, please e-mail SpecialMarkets@ ThomasNelson.com.

Library of Congress Cataloging-in-Publication Data

Library of Congress Control Number: 2018930397

ISBN 978-1-595541246
ISBN 978-1-595541284 (eBook)

Dedication

To the people of Platt Park Church,

You have touched me deeply. My heart has been shaped by your presence, your struggles, your faith, your questions, and your love. I've seen Jesus more because of you. As your pastor, my deepest desire has never been for you to form a strong bond with me or with this church — although it would be great if you did! Rather, my most earnest prayer has been that you would develop a deep, ongoing, personal connection with the Living God whose love for you has no limit. I hope you will come to know Him and experience His presence and guidance in your daily lives. I want the strongest anchor of your life to be tethered to Christ — not to me, our church, or any other substitute. I pray for His grace to be guiding you, His love securing you, His voice speaking to you, and His Holy Spirit flowing through you both during the difficult storms and the stunning sunsets of your life. My job as your pastor, and our role as a faith community, is simply to point you to

Christ. I hope to encourage you in the practices that strengthen your spirit. Our faith community — and all of its offerings — is a family for you, a spiritual gymnasium for the exercise of your soul. This is a place where you can practice growing in your faith through worship, prayer, community, communion, serving, and daily practices. Together, we are exercising the muscles of our faith, strengthening our desire for God and His kingdom to come here "on earth as it is in heaven" (Matthew 6:10 NIV).

Thank you for your love, for being in my life, and for being a church, my family, and a place I love to call home. Thank you for embracing Tim and I as your pastors. Serving you has been (and is!) one of the greatest joys of my life.

> *"And this is my prayer: that your love may abound more and more in knowledge and depth of insight, so that you may be able to discern what is best and may be pure and blameless for the day of Christ, filled with the fruit of righteousness that comes through Jesus Christ—to the glory and praise of God."*
> *(Phil 1:9-11)*

All my love and far more of His,

Table of Contents

PART 1

Embracing Life

*"Now choose life, so that you
and your children may live"*
(Deuteronomy 30:19)

*"How we spend our days is, of course,
how we spend our lives."*
— Annie Dillard, *The Writing Life*

Look at the Birds

The wild geese of Denver came from Canada and have not left, so I have a front row seat to watching geese every day as I walk our city parks and meander through the streets of our historic neighborhood. The geese make a mess, honk when they are angry, and stop traffic as they unselfconsciously cross the road at their own pace. Sometimes they sleep in the sun, or float in the water, or waddle about together.

It's a universal dream to fly like a bird, to 'soar on wings like eagles" into the heavens. Most days I don't feel like I am soaring. I feel more like I am trudging through a swamp of emails, meetings, meal prep, and child care. Jesus points to the birds of the air as an example to follow in order for our souls to flourish when He says, "Look at the birds, free and unfettered, not tied down to a job description, careless in the care of God. And you count far more to him than birds." (Matt. 6:26 MSG)

Flying is what you are made for. Birds in flight are a picture of freedom. The birds of the air rest and make a mess. They get angry and they sleep. And always, geese stick together in their iconic "V" pattern of flight. Martin Luther, in reflecting on the words of Jesus, said, "Let birds become your teachers."

Birds do the work of flapping their wings in taking flight and staying aloft. They rest in the soaring, taking advantage of the air currents beneath them. Flapping and soaring, alternating between the work and the rest through their days. That is the practice of a bird in flight, and it is an invitation to us to do the same. Flapping and soaring, sacrifice and renewal, creating and resting, labor and leisure. This is what we are made for. These rhythms are food for your soul.

Our souls long to live in the freedom that these birds know. It is thrilling, dangerous, breathtaking; a non-pretending, unhurried, unimaginable life. Jesus said, "Look at the birds of the air; they do not sow or reap or store away in barns, and yet your heavenly Father feeds them. Are you not much more valuable than they?" (Matt. 6:26)

So, are you ready to soar?

Planting Raspberry Bushes

Tim and I have planted raspberry bushes in three of our prior homes, although we have never lived at any of them long enough to enjoy the fruit. Now, we are thinking of planting some berry bushes again, but we don't want to jinx ourselves. We'd like to stay in this new house more than two minutes.

Gardening endeavors highlight the importance of seasons in our growth and productivity. Some Christian cultures tend to measure spiritual maturity by how much people do. The other day, someone said to me, "When I'm at church, I feel like a shmuck because everyone else is doing so much!" But activity is not how Jesus or the Bible talks about spiritual maturity. Instead, Jesus, the friend for all seasons, promises to meet us in the drought of summers, the cold of winters, the vibrancy of springs, and the rich harvest of autumns in our lives. God does not call us to a life of busyness, but rather to a life of fruitfulness. Paul says the fruit of the Spirit is love, joy, peace, patience, kindness, goodness, faithfulness, and self-control (Gal. 5:22–23).

Like any garden, our hearts can produce weeds as well as fruit. If we're not careful, the weeds of sin and shame will grow up in our hearts, choking out our spiritual life, and preventing us from bearing fruit (Mark 4:7). Part of our abiding fellowship with Christ means weeding the soil of our hearts. And weeding is a constant, tedious business.

The best way to get rid of weeds is to dig them up by the roots. Sometimes the roots of sin and shame run deep, have many branches, or break off beneath the surface, leading to regrowth. In the same way, we may have to deal with a particular sin more than once. Maybe many times. But we're encouraged that "If we confess our sins, he is faithful and just and will forgive us our sins and purify us from all unrighteousness" (1 John 1:9). Therefore, we rest in Jesus even while we keep watch over our hearts. What's happening in our lives that might become fertilizer for weeds? "Above all else, guard your heart, for everything you do flows from it." (Prov. 4:23)

I long for my life and for our church to replace the paradigm of busy spirituality with a spirituality of abiding. Abiding means that sometimes we are busy, and sometimes we are still. Sometimes we are pushing with all we've got, and other times we are just waiting patiently. Each season calls us to something different, and the real measure of maturity is not busyness, but rather the fruit our lives produce. Spiritual maturity calls us to the steady, quiet work of tending to our hearts as we pay attention to the Holy Spirit's wisdom and conviction so that God's character (the fruit of the Spirit) has room to flourish.

In reality, even fruitfulness can be difficult to observe or measure. Gardening of all kinds requires not only the discipline of weathering the seasons but also trusting that God will be faithful with the results.

The Grass Is Always Greener

You've heard it said, "The grass is always greener on the other side," but the truth is, the grass is greener where you water it.

We live in a world that constantly encourages us to compare and contrast our lives. Advertisements bombard us daily with images of what others have that we don't — but we could. So, we compete with our neighbors, envy our friends, and spend our energy trying to attain what others have. Our culture tells us that we never have enough, and, on some level, we believe we are always one acquisition away from happiness. We live like the hamster on a treadwheel, always spinning with new desires and dissatisfied energy, wanting what someone else already has.

But contentment is about cherishing what I already have, watering the grass of my own lawn. When I allow my thoughts to be consumed with what someone else has that I don't have, I am watering my neighbor's lawn. If I do this for too long, my own lawn will die. But when I focus on my own yard — water it, weed it, mow it, and fertilize it — then my own grass will become green. The Bible shows that contentment is associated with godliness, while loving and craving more can be the root of many sins (1 Tim. 6:6–10).

What part of your life is wilting from lack of attention? What action could you take today to care for your own lawn instead of watering someone else's? Where has discontentment crept in? What can you do to foster a growing contentment instead?

"The fear of the LORD leads to life; then one rests content, untouched by trouble."

(Prov. 19:23)

New Baby

Matt and Monika had their baby this week, and they brought him to church when he was just a few days old. When I saw baby Rockwell, I marveled at those little fingers and his tiniest button of a nose. Part of me wanted to freeze time for them, to somehow bottle up this newborn season and never let him grow up because he is so sweet and little and perfectly beautiful.

Our son, Russell, turns two years old this week. During these two years, we have eagerly awaited and embraced each of the "nexts" he has grown into. We were so excited when he could roll over, sit up, stand, walk on his knees (for a year), then walk on his tippy toes, and now run. A lot has changed in two years! So, when I saw baby Rockwell, I wanted to freeze time, not just for him, but also for Russell. Please, sweet baby love, stay small for a little longer because life goes so fast. Let your mama and daddy hold you and love you and snuggle you forever.

But we all know my wish is impossible. Soon there will be no stopping Rockwell from rolling and crawling and running. Even if Matt and Monika could slow his growth and hold him close to home for his whole life, would they? Probably not. They understand that a parent's role is not to keep our children small. The goal of parenting is to provide an environment of nurture and love so a child can grow up well. Even Jesus "grew in wisdom and in stature and in favor with God and all the people." (Luke 2:52 NLT)

Our responsibility is to point the way and provide the space so that our children can spread their wings, fly, and eventually soar. We get to show, tell, model, and teach (even in failures) what life with God looks like. We do this formally and informally as we go to church, sit at home, take a walk, sit at the breakfast table, and tuck them into bed (Deut. 6:4-7).

So, Matt and Monika and baby Rockwell and big boy Russell, may you never stop growing into His love and goodness for you. May you grow in the grace and knowledge of God, becoming a doer of good works in His name (2 Pet. 2:18; Eph. 2:10). May we, as your church family, provide the love and nurturing and space you need to become all God has designed you to be.

Adopting Lyla
Part 1

The dream of adopting a child has been in my heart for as long as I can remember. In second grade, I was obsessed with the movie *Annie*. At my *Annie*-themed birthday party that summer, I received an *Annie* album, an *Annie* necklace, and an *Annie* towel. The story of orphan Annie finding a home had captured me and everyone knew it. "Why adoption?" some people ask. I guess I just can't think of anything more beautiful in which to invest the life and resources God has given our family. It reflects the gospel itself. Through the death and resurrection of Christ, God adopts people into his family (Gal. 4:4–5).

When Tim and I first met in college, China had just opened up to Westerners and we were moved by the history, culture, and amazing people of China. Tim moved to Beijing for two years after college, serving with a ministry and teaching English. We were dating at the time, so I went to China to visit him. We have so many memories of that trip, including walking along the Great Wall of China, visiting Tiananmen Square, and eating super spicy noodles in a dingy underground restaurant. We were walking in Purple Bamboo Park when Tim brought up marriage. I said, "I'm really not ready for this conversation yet." Geez, what was I thinking?!

When we got married, we both agreed that starting a family "someday" was a desire of our hearts. We decided we would try "down the road" to have one child biologically and adopt one child from China.

Before our now three-and-a-half-year-old son, Russell, was even born, we had begun pursuing adoption through Chinese Children Adoption International. We filled out the application and attended the twenty-four hours of required parenting courses. Then, we sort of stalled out in completing all the paperwork. Part of our stalling out was just because neither of us is good at details, but I also think our hearts were catching up with all the realities of adoption. Eventually, our agency said we either needed to move forward or close our file.

With a lot of help and prayer, we finished the paperwork in the fall of 2014 and were finally "matched" with our soon-to-be daughter, Lyla, on January 8, 2015. We now wait for her to come home! We are filled with awe, wonder, anticipation, and a whole new set of hopes and fears as we await "Adoption Day."

> "The Spirit you received does not make you slaves, so that you live in fear again; rather, the Spirit you received brought about your adoption to sonship. And by him we cry, 'Abba, Father.'"
>
> (Rom. 8:15)

> "He predestined us for adoption to sonship through Jesus Christ, in accordance with his pleasure and will—"
>
> (Eph. 1:5 NLT)

Prioritizing My Marriage

Over the years, lots of people have asked Tim and me about working together, pastoring together, being landlords together. We have a lot of "together" going on! I'm a little sensitive when this topic comes up because it touches on all sorts of insecurities for me. Early in our marriage, we were told that spouses couldn't pastor together because it was nepotism and it would never work. Also, a lot of couples could not and should not work together, and I never want to send the impression that this model is for everyone. Finally, although we work together in a lot of domains right now, it might not always be what we want to do. I want to protect the choice for either or both of us to bow out or change vocational focus someday.

But, for now, Tim and I work together and we really like it. I see a side of Tim in our small business that I never knew he had until we started that venture. Who knew he was such an artist? We have both changed a lot in the five years we have co-pastored, and it's thrilling to be growth partners in ministry every day.

But co-leading and co-pastoring are not what make us married. Marriage is so much more than running a business or a household together. It's about writing a love story together. It's about walking hand in hand down the street for breakfast on a Monday morning — a pastor's Saturday! It is about surrendering my self-imposed need to cook every day and ordering carryout to eat on the front porch instead sometimes. It is about realizing that getting the dishwasher loaded can happen later, but some sort of daily investment in each other needs to happen every day. It is about giving up the urgent in favor of the important. Marriage is about making time for each other every day, small investments that add up over a lifetime. It is not about just talking business, although we do plenty of that. It is about talking and listening from your heart; hearing about the hopes, the fears, the dreams, and the mundane.

Tim and I have a lot of time together, but we have to fight for the kind of time that builds the sort of marriage we want to have. I think that's true for every couple, whether you work together or not. It's easy for us to just slip into business. Who's speaking? Who's watching Russell? When are we having those people over? Can I book that private event at the studio next month? Can I buy a new truck? (No! The answer to that last question is no.) There is a never-ending list of schedule-coordination, to-do lists, and logistics to discuss.

Today we talk about having "priorities" but, historically, the word "priority" was only ever used in the singular until very recently. In reality, you can only have one priority at a time. Keeping a priority is never easy. It means saying no to the good stuff in order to build the great stuff. Important relationships are worth prioritizing, but it will mean the laundry sometimes goes undone. It will mean eating leftovers so we don't give each other the leftovers of our attention and energy for another day.

Making one's marriage a priority is essential because marriage reflects the glory of God's love in the gospel of Christ. Paul says that marriage was created as a living picture of his love for His people (Eph. 5:22–33). Our willingness to humble ourselves and serve our spouse before others shows we understand what Jesus did for us. He did nothing out of "selfish ambition or vain conceit" (Phil. 2:3). Instead, He valued his bride, the Church, and put her needs and interests above His own, even laying down his life for her (Phil. 2:4–8). That is why keeping a marriage healthy not only honors the vows spoken at the wedding, it brings glory to Christ.

Morning Snuggles with Russell

I've loved Russell from the moment we became aware of his life inside of me. But there are moments lately when I look at him and the depth of love I feel nearly knocks me off my feet. The other day, he came into our bed early in the morning. Tim was already gone, and Russell lay there quietly holding my hand. The sweetness of his little fingers wrapped around mine, the features of his face, the warmth of his little body, the quietness of that moment, the stillness of early day all came together and made me want to weep in its beauty. In such moments, I think to myself, I would lay down in front of a train for you. I would learn how to fly for you. I would go anywhere, do anything, pay any price because I love you so much.

Then I think about God's love for me, and for you, and for Russell. I think about God's love for all people. For all the people He created. For all people of every nation, every political belief, every religious belief, and every status. All people, even annoying people and crazy people and irritating people, the ones who try so hard to be good and the ones who gave up on any attempts at goodness long ago. God created, He birthed all these beings, and His love for His creation is fierce.

I'm certain that Russell's three-year-old brain cannot fully comprehend or fathom the depths of my love for him. I'm certain that my little brain cannot fully grasp God's love for me either. But if my love for Russell is a fractured, incomplete, and imperfect picture of God's love for us, then the realization of the immensity of God's love changes everything. It makes me wonder...

Why would I ever fear in this sort of love?

Why would I ever embrace or support hatred or violence?

Why would I ever hold on to a grudge?

Why would I ever choose doing over being?

The list goes on and on.

The depth of Gods' love is an ever-deepening spiral, unfathomable, and it is our only context for enduring transformation and change. So, let's not be afraid to be like Russell and put our little hands in God's hands in the stillness and quiet and in the turmoil and terror of this life. We are loved.

"I have loved you with an everlasting love; I have drawn you with unfailing kindness."

(Jer. 31:3)

"For I am convinced that neither death nor life, neither angels nor demons, neither the present nor the future, nor any powers, neither height nor depth, nor anything else in all creation, will be able to separate us from the love of God that is in Christ Jesus our Lord."

(Rom. 8:38-39)

"And I pray that you, being rooted and established in love, may have power, together with all the Lord's holy people, to grasp

how wide and long and high and deep is the love of Christ, and to know this love that surpasses knowledge—that you may be filled to the measure of all the fullness of God."

(Eph. 3:17-19)

"But God demonstrates his own love for us in this: While we were still sinners, Christ died for us."

(Rom. 5:8)

You Watch Barney
and I'll Watch You

Last night, Russell picked up the Barney DVD that Nana brought him and said, "More, more, more!" I said, "You watch Barney and I'll watch you." The truth is, I enjoy watching him do just about anything (except maybe throw his food on the kitchen floor). While he sat on the floor enamored by the purple dinosaur, I sat enamored by my eighteen-month-old learning and laughing with Barney. Russell didn't even realize I was watching him; he was just doing what he does.

How do you imagine God is looking at you when you are doing whatever it is that you do (Ps. 139:1-12)? We probably don't realize how much God is not only watching us, but also enjoying watching us. Our loving God is not caught up in the tasks we're caught up in. He's much more caught up in the joy of His creation, just the essence and being of His beloved ones. Just like I don't need Russell to start performing, or

21

tying his shoes, or solving algebra equations, God doesn't need us to complete some important task to receive His love. He just loves to love.

I wonder how my view of God might change if I lived more in an awareness of His perfect love instead of trying to earn it, or deserve it, or prove that I'm worth it. Listen to Jesus who still calls out, "Come to me, all you who are weary and burdened, and I will give you rest. Take my yoke upon you and learn from me, for I am gentle and humble in heart, and you will find rest for your souls. For my yoke is easy and my burden is light." (Matt 11:28-30)

Dear Tim

Dear Tim,

I want to acknowledge, honor, and celebrate so many things about you this Father's Day. I am grateful for your tenderness, strength, funny ways, energy, insights, and love. But, maybe most of all, I'm grateful for your involvement in parenting. Sometimes our culture stereotypes dads as being uninvolved, aloof, oblivious, and disconnected, but you are nothing like that. You are every bit as involved in being Russell's dad as I am in being his mom. You are equally aware, tuned in, and committed. You prepare just as many meals, change just as many diapers, and say "no" or "maybe later" just as often as I do. I love that he can follow you around in the garage, swing with you, paint on canvas with you, and cook eggs for breakfast with you. I love watching the two of you together. I love raising Russell with you. I'm so glad you are his dad.

Happy Father's Day with love from us both,
Susie and Russell

Harvey the RV

I'm not really an RV person, but Tim has been daydreaming about our family owning one for a couple of years now. My daydreams usually involve a direct flight, a nice hotel, and drinks on the beach.

When Russell was just five weeks old (yes, you read that correctly, five *weeks* old), we took an RV vacation with our friends to CranFest in Wisconsin. Imagine this — me, Tim, our newborn, and our 85-lb sheepdog, plus Bill, Kate, and their two-year-old daughter, Mica, traveling through the night to view some cranberries growing in bogs. Dream vacation? Hardly. Memorable? Definitely.

For Tim, the RV represents family, togetherness, and memories. He gets all nostalgic and dreamy-eyed, imagining us road-tripping together some day. I've been on three RV trips in my life, and two involved breaking down on the side of the road. Our perspectives are definitely different!

But I love Tim and his enthusiasm is contagious. So, this week we actually pulled the trigger on a slightly used, twenty-one-foot RV for our family.

Sometimes love defers. Sometimes, love means moving to the other side or at least trying out the other perspective. Sometimes love says, "You know, that's not really my thing, but I'm happy to see you so happy. Let's give it a try." Sometimes love says, "If it's important to you, then it's important to me."

Practicing What I Preach

Our message series for Advent this past December was called "Be Present to the Unexpected." For four weeks leading up to our Christmas Eve services, I spoke about how unexpected it was for God to bring His son into the world as a baby. I taught that part of being present at Christmas time was being present to the unexpected things in our own lives. On Christmas Eve, I had a chance to practice what I preached.

Since Christmas Eve is the second-largest event of the church year, I always impose on myself some pressure for the services/message. All December long, I battle voices in my head that say, "Don't mess up this message because there will be a lot of visitors that day." And then I remind myself it's about God and not about me. I basically repeat this debate a hundred times in my head throughout the month.

The week before this Christmas, our nanny, Gabby, returned to China to visit her family after two years here in the US. We were so happy and excited for her, but her travel disrupted what had become our normal routines with our two-and-a-half-year-old son, Russell.

Our dear friend, Charlie, heard we needed help and volunteered to watch Russell for us on Christmas Eve morning. Around noon, I was in my office putting final touches on the talk for that afternoon when I got a call from Charlie saying Russell was sick. I zipped home, a conveniently short commute since we live next door to the church. Russell did not look good. By two o'clock, my concern hadn't waned, so I called the nurse hotline to get some advice and was told to bring him in right away. The only appointment was at three, and our first service was at 3:30 p.m. I was thinking, T minus 90 minutes until the service starts. No pressure here, Susie. Second-biggest event of the year, and your baby needs to go to the doctor!

I hung up the phone and started crying uncontrollably. Something about that mix of the pressure of a big day, my baby needing me, a little bit of the mother-guilt over having a babysitter on Christmas Eve, and the fear of what might be wrong with him resulted in my feeling raw, vulnerable, and all alone. So I cried big tears that seemed, even to me in the moment, a bit disproportionate for the situation, but I couldn't help it.

And then I got to practice being present to the unexpected — the unexpected sick kid, the unexpected tears, the unexpected timing of it all. God showed up for me in the unexpected presence of Rob and Carol (our medical expert friends and church elder) who came to our home, assessed and treated Russell, and reassured me. The blessing of their gift of love to me in that moment cannot be overstated. They were, hands down, the best Christmas gift I received, and they gave it just by being there and being Jesus-with-skin-on for me that day, the incarnational presence of Christ in my moment of need.

God also showed up for me in the unexpected presence of Curtis. Our professional musician friend canceled his Christmas Eve plans to stay with our son, skipping out on the candlelight service himself. He was away from his family for the first time ever on Christmas, and he chose to be family to us by sitting with our sick toddler. When I walked in our back door after the services were done, weary and grateful that God had gotten us through, Russell was curled up and sleeping on Curtis's lap on the couch. That image, even to this day, makes me weep.

Of all the plans we made that year for Christmas, God came closest to me in the unexpectedness of that night, which I will not soon forget.

The Hardest Thing to Do

I'm an extrovert, so I'm rarely short on words. But this week, God is asking me to hold my tongue, and I have to say it's the hardest thing for me to do. Not just a little hard like drinking my full eight glasses of water each day, but hard like everything within me is roaring to speak. I want to make myself understood and justify my position. Instead, I know I just have to walk away and be silent, living with being misunderstood and mistaken. It means trusting God instead of my ability to explain and fix.

Let me fill you in. I chose to have one of those "can I share my experience of you recently?" conversations with a dear friend. I stayed up late the night before, praying and journaling about exactly what to say. Having the conversation was a risk, and I wasn't looking forward to it. But there have been a few times when others have taken this risk with me, and this kind of conversation has been the most loving gift I could have been offered. I know how important it can be. Direct feedback from someone who knows you and loves you (very key, not talking about angry critics here) is an exceptionally rare and precious gift.

But the conversation with my friend didn't go so well. For whatever reason, she couldn't receive my feedback — I've been there before too. She deflected, minimized, sabotaged, and turned dramatic, enlisting another person to "her side of the story" almost immediately.

So, here lies my fork in the road. I could try again, explain my perspective, and attempt to make myself understood. Or, I could turn on her, go toxic, and get caustic. Either way would mean more talking. And, for the first time in a long time, silence seems like the only good and right option.

So much of what I do day-to-day depends on words. Yet, sometimes, wisdom and character lie not in what we say but in what we don't say. "Those who guard their lips preserve their lives, but those who speak rashly will come to ruin" (Prov. 13:3). Sometimes, the best thing to do is to just get quiet and walk away. Sometimes we need to be like David in the Bible, who chose not to retaliate when he was being unjustly attacked. When Saul threw spears at David, he didn't break out his bow, rally his troupes, or fight back. Instead he fled, alone and silent (1 Sam. 18:11; 19:8–18).

I know I have to be quiet for now. And being silent is the hardest thing to do. It's requiring me to trust God with the outcome when I'd so much rather try to control it on my own. But the Lord says to me, "Be still, and know that I am God" (Ps. 46:10).

On the Edge of Forevermore

The other day, I met with a couple whose marriage is totally on the edge. In their case, the passion is gone and they've grown distant. They believe it's unlikely that their relationship will survive. I have known them for a long time and care about them deeply. My heart breaks over their situation.

My heart breaks partly because I believe in redemption, and I've witnessed its surprising grace in marriage. That grace comes in many different ways, sometimes through fighting and staying and rediscovering intimacy, and other times through trying every resource and ultimately leaving (possibly for reasons of personal safety — physical, emotional, mental, and/or spiritual).

But I worry about the prevalence of people who seem to shortcut the potential for redemption in marriage. Many are turning away from each other because they no longer experience pleasure, delight, or intimacy together anymore. Certainly, these are painful developments, and they demand attention and care in marriage, but I grieve over the flippancy with which our culture offers marital breakup as an acceptable solution.

I asked my friends who are contemplating divorce a question I've asked a hundred times before, "Have you been to counseling?" Their response, like a hundred others I've heard before, was, "We looked into that, but it's too expensive, and we are so busy."

I wanted to say to them, "Seriously? Too expensive? Too time consuming? I don't mean to lose my cool here, but think this through. You are considering divorce. Do you know how expensive that is? Do you realize how time consuming that will be? Please, please do not enter that path lightly. I know sometimes divorce is the only option left, and there are solid reasons for people to split up. But I implore you to try every good resource first. Leave no stone unturned in your attempt to reconcile. Give redemption a fighting chance!"

During our third year of marriage, Tim and I hit an extremely rough patch. It was scary for both of us to experience the intensity of emotions, to see such an ugly side of ourselves and each other. I remember in the midst of that painful season, I called a friend and told her we were really struggling. We talked, she listened, and then offered me one of the most generous gifts in that season. She had an amazing counselor who was difficult to get in to see, but she'd be willing to give up her upcoming session if we would be willing to drive the three hours to see him. Without skipping a beat, we said yes. We drove three hours each way multiple times and paid money on top of that to see this man. I'm so grateful we did, and I can undoubtedly say it was worth every penny and all the time it took.

So, I hope you will forgive me when I grow weary of hearing, "It's too expensive," or "We just don't have time." If this is your situation today, hear my urgency, which comes from love. Make time. Find the money. Because there is no price too high and no time investment too great to do all you can to save your marriage. God is the great Redeemer, but we often get to participate in that process through the choices we make, which can have a forevermore impact.

If you don't know who to see, email me. If you truly cannot find a way to pay, email me. Just don't let time and money be the reasons you walk away from giving your marriage every chance to succeed.

* If you have experienced a divorce you regret, know that God's pleasure and delight in you has not changed and He still has unlimited capacity for redemption. Our mistakes never cancel out God's mercy and the potential for Him to work beauty, goodness, and healing in and through our lives.

The Average CEO

The average tenure of a Fortune 500 CEO is just 4.6 years, and it's even shorter for many pastors (four years). This statistic could be explained by burnout, but it could also be a reflection of a shadowy tendency of human nature. People sometimes leave when the going gets tough, when the honeymoon is over. By changing positions frequently, it's possible to keep one's life and leadership in a constant "honeymoon phase" and leave the problems to someone else. However, this isn't the kind of leadership Jesus modeled and advocated.

Jesus talked once about the mentality of the shepherd versus the hired hand. He said, "The hired hand is not the shepherd and does not own the sheep. So when he sees the wolf coming, he abandons the sheep and runs away. Then the wolf attacks the flock and scatters it" (John 10:12). The shepherd has ownership of his flock. He's invested in their well-being and connected with their destiny. Jesus describes himself as "the Good Shepherd" who knows His sheep and lays His life down for them (John 10:11). When it comes to that which God calls us to do, He wants us to imitate Jesus and be shepherds/owners, not hired hands.

Although it has taken me some time, I'm now grateful for a leadership crisis I experienced at an early age. I had to face my own inclination to run away. I experienced new levels of grace through the grueling, soul-refining work of conflict resolution, forgiveness, and team building that test a leader's character. Crisis, portrayed in Jesus' parable as the wolf's intrusion and attack, has a way of revealing motives and prompting reactive behavior. We all have a mix of pure and impure, selfish and loving motives, but crisis often strips us of our facades and exposes to us what is really important. It clarifies why we are doing what we are doing and to what extent we are committed to the "sheep" entrusted to us. It can be a tremendous way to grow in intimacy with the Lord and mature our faith (James 1:2–4).

Martin Luther King, Jr. once said, "The ultimate measure of a man is not where he stands in moments of comfort and convenience, but where he stands at times of challenge and controversy." *Strength to Love*, reprint (Minneapolis, MN: Fortress, 2010), 26. 1963[1]

When crisis comes, let's trust our Jesus-shepherd and be faithful to the task and people who look to us for leadership. Let's allow hard times to take us deeper with the One who loves us and gave His life for us. Our Great Shepherd promises to equip us with "everything good for doing his will." (Heb. 13:20)

---

[1] *Strength to Love*, reprint (Minneapolis, MN: Fortress, 2010), 26. 1963

It's My Birthday

Today is my birthday, and I'm thirty-seven. I know some of you are thinking, "Wow, she's old!" while others may be thinking, "I remember when I was that young." Age is what it is and there's no changing it, no matter how much Botox, mommy make-over work, and age-defying moisturizers are applied. Honestly, I kind of hesitated to tell my age because I know it could discredit me one way or the other, depending on who you are and where you find yourself on the age spectrum in relation to me. The Scriptures say, "And don't let anyone put you down because you're young. Teach believers with your life: by word, by demeanor, by love, by faith, by integrity" (1 Tim. 4:12 MSG). Paul, Timothy's mentor and the author of these words, was apparently familiar with our human tendency to size up ourselves and others by artificial rubrics of maturity. He gave Timothy a different and wholly counter-cultural measuring tool, the quality of a person's character and life legacy.

I've had a front row seat to some people who have not handled the changes of aging well. I also know some people who are aging well and without fear of rejection. When I say "aging well," I don't mean they look twenty at forty, per se, but rather they are more alive, content, in touch with their heart, confident, and free at forty than they did at twenty. Their lives, by word, demeanor, love, faith, and integrity reveal an inner depth and stability. And I just have to say, that is really beautiful to see. Grey hair grown through the courage of risking to love and wrinkles acquired through daring to still laugh in the midst of pain trump perfect hair and flawless skin in my book.

My birthday prayer today is for each of us to grow in grace as we age, no matter how many years we count.

I Got Carded!

Tonight I got carded! I share that with great enthusiasm because, when you're an almost-forty-year-old mom of a toddler and you're no longer pulling off the Forever 21 wardrobe, getting carded feels like a real compliment! Can I get a witness?

I'm surprised by how happy it made me to think some random stranger (whose job it is to ask for IDs) may have momentarily thought I was closer to twenty than forty. I do, sometimes, miss the spontaneity, energy, and adventure of youthfulness. Those days were awfully fun!

Usually, I don't mind that I'm getting older. I respect and admire many individuals who truly seem much more grounded and beautiful to me at fifty, sixty, seventy, and eighty than I ever remembering myself or my friends being at twenty-something-and-still-finding-the-way.

The lines on my older friends' faces and the wrinkles on their hands have been acquired through living and loving and fighting. Those age markers have been earned through the crucible of life, the hodgepodge of bitter and sweet moments. That kind of beauty, born from surviving and thriving, is lovelier to me than skinny jeans and perfect skin any day.

Our recent study on heaven has taught me that, in glory, our bodies will be fully restored. I wonder what that will be like? We won't be ghosts, bobbing six inches above the ground. We will be ourselves, in our own skin, with two feet on the ground, walking, dancing, kissing and hugging other real people. We will be healthy, whole, and filled with joy.

Maybe that flicker of pleasure in being carded tonight points to my soul's hope that heaven is really true. Maybe I have in me a subconscious echo of a future in eternity where aging and worry and feelings of inadequacy and aching and tears and troubles will be no more. C.S. Lewis said, "Heaven is the music we were born hearing." Maybe eternity is written in our hearts more than we know. Or maybe, I just like getting carded because what almost-forty-year-old woman doesn't? Either way, I join the apostle Paul in eagerly awaiting that day when God will make all things, including our aging, failing bodies, new.

Singing to Russell

Every night, I sing to Russell before tucking him in bed. Usually, I ask him what song he wants to hear and most nights he requests "Santa Baby," a made-up story or song about Papa Bear, or a song about his friends, Benji and Claire. One night recently, though, he said, "Mommy and Daddy drink wine, I drink juice." True confession, that is what my three-year-old requested I sing about! You'll have to imagine how that song turned out because you'll never hear it from me. No matter what I sing with Russell, I almost always end the night with a hymn, and lately it has been "Come Thou Fount."

This past summer, we did a message series called "Wisdom of the Hymnal." In it, we looked at the stories and meanings behind some of the ancient hymns, including "Come Thou Fount." One of the great lines says, "Tune my heart to sing thy grace."

I love that line because it sounds like a prayer of invitation rather than of obligation. Sometimes I engage in spiritual practices from a sense of obligation or duty. And practices may legitimately become routine disciplines of daily life. But I don't like when I find myself living primarily out of duty. We always have freedom to offer our spiritual practices with a whispered prayer that says, "Lord, in this practice, tune my heart to sing thy grace." Embodying God's grace is, after all, one of the healthy purposes of investing myself in spiritual practices. While my participation may delight God, it certainly nourishes my own spirit and hopefully bears witness of God's aliveness and relevance.

A few spiritual practices have become meaningful to me lately. The first is the spiritual practice of slowing, in which I put my feet flat on the floor and take several deep breaths in and out. Tune my heart to your perspective and pace, Lord. Next is the spiritual practice of reading, in which I aim for depth over breadth. Tune my heart to your deep mind and heart, God. Last is the spiritual practice of friendship, in which I make time for eyeball-to-eyeball, face-to-face, unhurried time with someone else. Tune my heart to being present over perfect, Lord, available and wholly right here, right now.

Through each of these, I am learning to whisper a simple request, "Lord, tune my heart."

Why Facebook Isn't Enough

Tim and I recently sat through two eight-hour days of parenting classes in preparation for our upcoming adoption. In a required class about attachment, we learned the distinction between bonding and attaching. Bonding activities lead to attachment, and attachment is fundamental to a child's development. Bonding activities for new parents include things like holding, singing, making eye contact and all the goo-goo-ga-ga babbling that new parents do with their babies. We were encouraged to prioritize and participate in a variety of bonding activities with our adopted child in the hope of forming a strong attachment, which will be critical to every step of our journey together.

I came home from our training sessions and prepared for Platt Park Church's present sermon series, called "Alone: If We Never Learn to Be Alone, All We'll Ever Be Is Lonely." My preparation included reading about Facebook's impact on society, and this quotation from an article in the *Atlantic Daily* struck me: "What Facebook has revealed about human nature — and this is not a minor revelation — is that a connection is not the same thing as a bond." A connection is not the same as a bond, and a bond is not the same thing as an attachment.

Facebook is more about connections than bonding. Bonding usually happens face to face in those moments when we can't easily project or edit an image of ourselves. Over time, enough of these unedited face-to-face bonds form attachments between people. But this kind of meaningful attaching requires us to get off our devices and actually make time and space for face-to-face encounters.

When God created Adam, the first man, He said, "It is not good for the man to be alone." But Adam was not alone; Adam was with God! Apparently, even God's presence was not enough to fully satisfy Adam's heart, and so God created companionship. God knew that humans would need "face time" with other people to survive and grow.

I'm a fan of Facebook, but I want to guard myself from the illusion that all my quick little connections are creating or sustaining healthy, vibrant attachments. Absolutely nothing can replace the gift of being present to each other in time and space.

Who are you intentionally connecting with?

Who has gifted you with their presence? How responsive have you been?

How are you creating space in your life for genuine, face-to-face moments that help create bonds?

The Jade Plant

Several years ago, I had a really huge, old jade plant. When people walked into my office, they often commented, "Cool plant!" A guy from Texas came to our office once, and he loved my jade plant so much that I chopped off a big portion for him to take home and repot. In fact, I cut off big branches of that jade several times and shared them with people who later told me their new plant was thriving.

The church I was serving at the time went through a very difficult season, and ironically, as the ministry began to shrivel and struggle, my jade plant seemed to lose its vibrancy too. After a few months, my jade plant wasn't looking so good. It had gone from healthy and robust to limp and lifeless. When the jade plant finally fell and the once mighty plant was declared dead, I began the cleanup process. A few green leaves remained and still appeared to be growing, but I was shocked to discover that the inside of the jade's trunk was completely rotten!

This is actually a common problem for the jade plant. When watering habits or its environment changes, the soil can be overloaded with moisture, allowing a fungus to grow. The root of the plant is attacked by the fungus and begins to rot from the inside out. Something similar can happen to us as well. When we begin to take holiness lightly and expose ourselves to more of sin's influence, we can find it beginning to attack our souls. Like the Pharisees, we may look great on the outside, but be rotting on the inside (Matt. 23:26-28).

What we see on the outside is not always consistent with what's on the inside. Sometimes people, families, organizations, and endeavors look very good, very "up and to the right," but in reality, the middle is rotten. Sometimes, a rotten middle comes in the form of a narcissistic leader at the helm, the mismanagement of resources, or perhaps disgruntled staff. Rotten middles always reveal themselves in time, and they always bring death and destruction. That's why interior health must be a priority for leaders, families, churches, and businesses.

Scripture tells us, "Guard your heart, for it is the wellspring of life" (Prov. 4:23). We are well into this new week, and there is no time like the present to do the difficult work of examining our hearts before God and taking whatever steps are needed to participate with God in our healing and renewing. If you are unsure where to begin, try this simple process:

1. Be still with God. Examine the jade plant of your life. Not just the exterior leaves that everyone sees and admires, but also the inner thoughts, emotions, and motivations where sin begins and temptations lie (James 1:14-5).

2. If any part of this slow examination causes you shame or sadness, notice it.

3. Sit with the noticing, as if you are looking deep into the core of the jade plant, seeing the colors, feeling the textures, maybe smelling the stench.

4. If needed, confess your "rotten middle" and your need for God's help. When we cover our sin, the burden is heavy (Ps. 34:4). But

God promises to forgive when we acknowledge our sin before Him (Ps. 34:5; 1 John 1:9).

5. Ask God for wisdom to know what steps may be needed.
6. Make a movement in the direction of healing and restoration.

PART 2

Passages

There is a time for everything, and a season for every activity under the heavens: a time to be born and a time to die, a time to plant and a time to uproot, a time to kill and a time to heal, a time to tear down and a time to build, a time to weep and a time to laugh, a time to mourn and a time to dance, a time to scatter stones and a time to gather them, a time to embrace and a time to refrain from embracing, a time to search and a time to give up, a time to keep and a time to throw away, a time to tear and a time to mend, a time to be silent and a time to speak, a time to love and a time to hate, a time for war and a time for peace. What do workers gain from their toil? I have seen the burden God has laid on the human race. He has made everything beautiful in its time. He has also set eternity in the human heart; yet no one can fathom what God has done from beginning to end.

—Ecclesiastes 3: 1–11

A Story for You

Anyone's story...

At the dinner party, she mingled with new acquaintances. "What do you do for a living?" they asked.

She replied, "Oh, I do several things," and she launched into her list of various jobs.

"Wow, that's amazing, I don't know how you do so much!"

Deep inside, she felt a twinge of sadness. What made her amazing in their eyes and in her own eyes wasn't who she was so much as what she did. The admiration, the definition, the wow factor wasn't about the honest, internal stuff. It was about the external. It wasn't about joyfulness, kindness, and generosity. It was about juggling responsibilities, keeping plates spinning, and never crying about it.

It wasn't their fault for marveling. She pushed, hustled, worked hard, proved her worth, achieved countless life goals, and pleased others — all to avoid pain. Addiction does that. It masks the pain. Her addiction to proving she could do it all masked painful questions. Will I be invited, included, and loved if I don't prove myself? Am I worthy of love and belonging if I don't get a lot of stuff done? Even tonight, she felt the questions pulsing behind her smiles and charming conversations with other guests.

My story...

The woman in the story above sounds a lot like me not too long ago. Then I turned forty, and everything shifted. I didn't experience a shift in schedule, time management, or vocation. But I had a new realization about what was inside. The old way of living had left me feeling exhausted, frantic, disconnected, and lonely. I needed a new way that wasn't about proving my worth.

I started to delve into what "wholeness" could mean in my life. Wholeness meant mindful attentiveness rather than constant achieving. It meant being okay with letting people down at times. I have slowly, carefully stopped reporting to everyone who asks me for anything and have begun reporting to the still small voice within. When that voice says rest, I drive to the mountains and temporarily ignore email. When that voice says it is time for a family day, I leave my work undone and go home to the people I love.

The shift isn't easy, and it isn't complete. The shape of it might look different for others in different circumstances, but when I honor this invitation from God, it is freedom and peace and life. Some days are two steps forward and three steps back, but inside I sense a fundamental change to my value structure; my longings and motivations have shifted.

Before, busyness and hard work were always the best way through. Now rest, quiet, and connection are usually the best way forward. Before, what I did defined me. Now, my worthiness and value are more rooted in being a beloved child of God. I am learning to live like I cannot lose favor.

Epilogue...

People called her amazing for what she juggled, and she kept juggling. But today, she is creating something different and beautiful that cannot be seen but feels so much more grounded and true.

"We proclaim to you what we have seen and heard, so that you also may have fellowship with us. And our fellowship is with the Father and with his Son, Jesus Christ."

(1 John 1:3)

"But when the kindness and love of God our Savior appeared, he saved us, not because of righteous things we had done, but because of his mercy. He saved us through the washing of rebirth and renewal by the Holy Spirit, whom he poured out on us generously through Jesus Christ our Savior."

(Titus 3:4-6)

Dear Russell

Dear Russell,

I am a blubbering mess. I just cannot seem to stop crying. Every time I think about leaving for this trip to China to pick up your sister, Lyla, I find myself in a puddle of tears. It's not the fact that I won't see you for two weeks, though that will be hard. The reason for my tears is I know when I say goodbye to you and board that plane, I am saying goodbye to an era with you; a very special season of life when you have been my one and only baby, and we have been a family of just three. That season is coming to a close and it's sad to say goodbye.

This time with you has been so special. I remember when we found out about you. You were the size of a sesame seed inside of me. I remember the day we brought you home from the hospital, the moment you took your first step, and the first time you said, "I love you too, Mommy." These memories and countless more, I hold in my heart as priceless gifts. I love being your mom.

Maybe I am grieving the changes that will come as you continue to grow up. This whole grieving thing is no joke, evidenced by my constant crying. Whew! In these moments, life's pains seem to teach my heart new depths. Right now, before God, I am remembering that you're not mine. Oh, I talk about you like you're my child, but ultimately you're not. You belong to God, and you are a gift to me. You have been entrusted to my care. It's one of the greatest honors, privileges, and joys of my entire life. But ultimately, you lie in the hand of a great God who loves to give good gifts.

Jesus keeps inviting me to let go and die a little. Leaving this season with you, relinquishing this era, feels like a little death. I want to freeze time and never let this go, never let you go, never have to hear you say, "Hold me, Mommy" for the last time, never have to wave goodbye as one of us leaves the other. But Jesus keeps beckoning me to let go, to relinquish control, and remember that you are in His ultimate care. He keeps reminding me that even you, dearest Russell, cannot — must not — take the place of God in my life. It is only in holding all my wonderful gifts from God lightly, acknowledging that they never really were mine to clutch, that I can experience the freedom, joy, and life found in God. I so much want you to know that God truly is the best gift life holds, even better than my love for you, or Daddy's and my love for each other, or any other beautiful gift you or I can imagine.

I love you, Russell, more than I ever realized I could. You are a gift from God to me, and I'm so grateful! When we sing, "He's got the whole world in His hands," that includes you, me, Daddy, Lyla, and this sweet season we have shared.

I love you, honey,
Mommy

Saying Goodbye to Sam

"The dog was created specially for children. He is the god of frolic."

—Henry Ward

I was never much of a dog person until we got our Old English Sheepdog. We named him Samwise Gamgee, after Frodo's best friend, since he was about to become our family's new best friend. Tim and I were living in Iowa, and I was sad and resistant about being in a town that felt way too small for my ambitious twenty-something-year-old heart. I traveled a lot for work, flying in and out of Chicago, so we had Sam shipped from a breeder in Montana and picked him up in the cargo section of O'Hare International airport after one of my work trips.

I was instantly in love. That seventy-pound, fluffy puppy sat on my lap the whole three-hour drive home to our house on the Mississippi River in Iowa.

Sam settled gently into our lives during that tough season when our marriage was being tested in new ways, my faith was being strengthened, and I was discovering that hope really is stronger than my fears. Sam was a great comic relief for us in the midst of all the loneliness, tension, struggle, and tears twelve years ago.

Since that first day, Sam has been a constant presence and has moved with us eight times. He was there to welcome our son home from the hospital. He watched and comforted us through Russell's many firsts and our parenting firsts. From Sam, we learned about the value of play and companionship, rhythm and routine.

Over the last few months, we noticed Sam losing his energy and his ability to walk. We watched as he grew increasingly uncomfortable. We slowly and reluctantly recognized that Sam was dying.

Earlier this week, we had to say goodbye to Sam. I cannot remember the last time I cried this much! Even though his health had been declining for some time, nothing prepared us for saying goodbye to a dog that had become family. We miss him already. We're so grateful for the special years God gave us with our fluffy puppy. A friend shared this quote from author Milan Kundera, which sums up one of the many gifts God gave us through Sam: "Dogs are our link to paradise. They don't know evil or jealousy or discontent. To sit with a dog on a hillside on a glorious afternoon is to be back in Eden, where doing nothing was not boring — it was peace."

Sam, we love you, and we are so glad God gave you to our family. You will forever be in our hearts.

The Tunnel of Chaos

There is a tunnel called chaos. Have you ever been in it? It's a place where you get lost in the feeling of never enough — never enough time, never enough resources, never enough support, never enough people, never enough. This tunnel makes you feel like you are running, running, running without an end in sight. Sometimes it seems like maybe you could try to step out of the race for a minute, but then you immediately think, *Who would I be? And how would I know if I were worthy of love and belonging?* All of your life you've proven your worth through striving and performing. You are capable, you are talented, you are strong. You've got this, you've always got this.

In the beginning, it was fun. You felt a surge of energy, being able to offer something of value to the world. But over time it felt more like an addiction than a calling, and now it's just a habit. You live busy, driven, preoccupied, isolated, addicted. Addicted to outcomes, to work, to an image of perfection. Perfect leader, perfect parent, perfect online profile, perfect life. You don't like to admit it, but you're addicted to proving your worth through performance. When people ask, "How are you doing?" you answer, "Busy," and if they probe further, you really don't know the answer.

Of course, it's not always that way. Moments of honesty, vulnerability, and truth make you long for more. The tunnel of chaos that initially felt so thrilling has become increasingly dissatisfying. You want something truer, less forced, less phony. You want to shed the racing gear that has served you well through your twenties and maybe your thirties, but it is hard and scary because who will you be without those clothes? Will you be enough without the pretending and performing? What if people think you're a slacker? And since all the running involves using and sharing your "spiritual gifts," would it be spiritually irresponsible to slow down?

This conundrum is part of growing up. Most lives are divided into two parts. We begin building a sense of who we are and striving for our place in this world. Eventually, we see this isn't enough and enter the second half of life where the purpose in life is about more than safety and security. Richard Rohr said, "Unless you somehow 'weep' over your own phoniness, hypocrisy, and wounded-ness, you probably will not let go of the first half of life."

Maturity feels like leaving our false selves for our true selves. Maturity involves leaving the tunnel of chaos filled with rat races and hamster wheels to enter the unknown land of your good and worthy self in Christ. Discipleship includes realizing that you were born worthy of love and belonging, not because of what you can do, but because of who you are. It takes courage and daring to live with your whole heart wide open to God, without any pretense or performance, but the gifts of such vulnerability are rest and contentment.

Adopting Lyla
Part 2

When we said "yes" to adopting Lyla, her caregiver posted a photo on Facebook with the words, "I am chosen."

I couldn't help but think of how Jesus says, "I have chosen you," and how often I take that as a pressuring message. You're chosen, blessed, redeemed. So, get busy serving meals and hosting groups and working hard in the church. Your duty as a chosen one is to be responsible and pay back the gift you've been given in being chosen.

Then I think about Lyla. My mama-heart jumped for joy when I saw the picture of her sweet little face next to the words "I am chosen." I wanted to reach through the computer screen and say, "Yes, you are chosen, sweet baby girl," and hold her in my arms. I want Lyla to know that, as her imperfect mom, I care infinitely more about her being than her doing. I hope for her to be brave, to be free, to be true, to be

God-honoring. Whatever she does out of that center is just by-product. It doesn't matter to me if she does anything great in the world's eyes.

Maybe God sees us the same way.

Imagine a photograph of yourself. God looks at your face and is overwhelmed with delight. You are chosen.

"This is what the LORD says—he who created you, Jacob, he who formed you, Israel: 'Do not fear, for I have redeemed you; I have summoned you by name; you are mine. When you pass through the waters, I will be with you; and when you pass through the rivers, they will not sweep over you. When you walk through the fire, you will not be burned; the flames will not set you ablaze. For I am the LORD, your God, the Holy One of Israel, your Savior; I give Egypt for your ransom, Cush and Seba in your stead. Since you are precious and honored in my sight, and because I love you.'" (Isaiah 43:1-4)

Dear Lyla

Hi friends! I've been super sentimental lately, getting ready for our trip to China to adopt Lyla. I've been writing letters to Lyla and Russell. I thought I would share this letter below with all of you, just out of gratitude for how our church family has been such an integral part of our family's life and journey. I see and understand the human adoption process to be a beautiful, if imperfect, analogy of the spiritual adoption God offers through Christ, and my hope and prayer is that, by sharing some of our journey, we might somehow encourage you along yours.

Dear Lyla,

I cannot wait to meet you! In just one week, you'll be in my arms. This will be one of the happiest days of my life and one of the saddest, most confusing days of yours. I daydream all the time about what meeting you will be like. I wonder if you'll be scared, happy, or aloof. I wonder if you'll smile or cry or run away or let me hold you close.

Whatever you do is okay. You just be you. Once we are with you, we aren't going anywhere. We are here to stay. We are adopting you. This means that you will be a Grade, and we will be a family. You will have a mommy and daddy, a brother named Russell, and a big fluffy dog named George. When you are sad, there will be people to hold you and comfort you and share your tears. When you are happy, there will be people to laugh with you and bear witness to your joys. When you are afraid, you don't have to be alone with your fears. Adoption means you're no longer alone. You have a family with whom you belong.

I hope with all my heart that your belonging to us and our belonging to you will someday introduce you to an even greater adoption into the family of God. As you grow, I hope you'll come to experience the eternal family of Father, Son, and Holy Spirit. Spiritual adoption offers us all a belonging that's infinitely deeper, richer, and kinder than our human family ever can. Being adopted into the family of God means living in the promise that Jesus will never leave you or forsake you. It means there are brothers and sisters and aunts and uncles and cousins and parents for you in every church community you choose to belong to throughout your life. There will be times when I am not the mother you need, and, in those moments, God may use a Sunday school teacher, a youth leader, or small group leader, pastor, or friend to "mother you". There will be times when you need a sister to share life with, and God will provide you with a sister-in-Christ to be by your side.

Some of my deep hopes and prayers for you are that you will know the marvelous experience of dancing in God's love, that you'll find your stride and identity as God's adopted child, and that you'll experience the awe and wonder of belonging to a church family. There is nothing like a church family when a church family is working right. No family is perfect, but there are lessons in belonging and depths of communion that I've only known in the presence of God and His people.

I cannot imagine my love for you being any greater than it is already. I see pictures of you and my arms ache to hold you. I watch videos of you and my heart leaps for joy. I have studied your little face, your curly hair, and every bit of information we have received about you so that it's burned into my mind and heart. You are loved so deeply already, and we haven't even met yet!

I am so honored, humbled, and excited about being your mom. I love you so much, and I'm counting down the days until we meet.

On Being Nice

Recently, our marriage counselor said to me, "Susie, you are very nice, and that is not a compliment." Ouch! That did not feel good. But, alas, it's true, I was raised in the Midwest and trained as a pastor, so I have a PhD in "nice-y nice." And I'm grateful for the honest feedback, which is a rare and precious gift indeed.

I'm realizing that nice is not the same as loving. Yes, I know I'm very late to the party in this realization. I guess I've known it in my head, but applying it to my life is another matter. Christ calls me to love, which may not always mean being nice. In fact, if I'm nice to your face and turn around and vent about you to someone else, I was anything but loving. Sometimes love calls for fierceness, and sometimes that intensity doesn't feel so nice.

So I'm pushing the reset button. I'm choosing a new way. It might be clunky for me, and I'm sure I will relapse, but with God's help, I choose to live in love and not just in nice.

Sacred and Scared

Think about this for a minute: scared and sacred have the exact same letters. I wonder if that's because scared and sacred are more related than we realize. Just this week, I was asked to speak at another church in town. I speak almost every week at our church, but when this invitation arrived, I felt scared. Immediately my mind started generating excuses. I really need to stay focused. I don't need anything else on my plate right now. My voice is not that unique anyway. But before saying no, I thought I had better pray about it. And when I got quiet and honest, I had to admit the main feeling behind my excuses was fear.

I wonder how often I miss the sacred because I'm hiding behind scared?

The good news is that God specializes in moving people from a scared place to sacred ground. Consider Hagar who ran from Sarah because she was afraid, but encountered God in the desert. God's instruction equipped her to return to the place she feared in order to carry out God's plans for Ishmael and Isaac. Consider Moses who was afraid to speak, yet later stayed alone with God on smoking Mount Hebron for forty days. God's counsel guided Moses in leading the Israelites. Consider Peter who denied Christ, responding out of his terror of being included in Christ's sufferings, yet, later, faith like his became the rock on which God built the church.

This week, I choose to relinquish my fear and trust God to make the sacredness. Will you do the same?

"So do not fear, for I am with you; do not be dismayed, for I am your God. I will strengthen you and help you; I will uphold you with my righteous right hand."

(Isaiah 41:10)

"You came near when I called you, and you said, 'Do not fear.'"
(Lamentations 3:57)

"Do not be afraid, little flock, for your Father has been pleased to give you the kingdom."
(Luke 12:32)

"Peace I leave with you; my peace I give you. I do not give to you as the world gives. Do not let your hearts be troubled and do not be afraid."
(John 14:27)

Batten Down the Hatches

Last summer, Tim and I picked up an old sailboat from Craigslist. The sailboat's name, *SoulMate*, is inscribed on its side. Now, we don't exactly know how to sail (which our friends love to tease us about), but we sure love trying and even just hanging out in the slip or motoring around Lake Dillon. Frisco Marina has become one of my favorite places to go be quiet and contemplative.

Today, I woke up insanely early and drove to Frisco to watch the sunrise from *SoulMate*. When I first arrived, it was forty-eight degrees. I had my hoodie up and I was bundled in blankets as I read, journaled, and prayed. It started to warm up, as it usually does, and pretty soon, I shed the hoodie and looked for ways to hide from the intensity of the Colorado sun. Then, without warning, clouds rolled in, unleashing a thunderstorm. I scrambled to "batten down the hatches" before my laptop got too wet. Waiting out the storm from inside, I watched the billowing clouds, listened to the pounding of rain, felt the rocking of the boat as the waves crashed against its sides, and smelled that combination of lake and storm. I rested happily and safely, soaking it all in.

Life's weather can change in a moment too. Sometimes you're doing great, full of joy and thankfulness, and then, out of nowhere, a wave of loneliness, grief, or deep soul fatigue can overtake you. Other times, despair presses against us so heavily that it seems we are trapped, and a ray of human kindness or natural beauty shocks us with hope. In every shifting season, God offers us Himself as our *SoulMate*.

God is able to calm the spiritual storms just as easily as the physical ones (Mark 4:39). But sometimes we must batten down the hatches of our lives and hide with Christ in God. In Him, we can have a peace which passes understanding (Phil. 4:7). This can mean refusing to be too busy for daily stillness. It can mean steeping ourselves in Scripture, or music, or outdoor beauty, or camping, or whatever nourishes and reminds us of God's deep and personal love for us. To live in the love of Christ is to live moment by moment, in season and out of season, in the knowledge of our belovedness in Him. God is our best *SoulMate*, the maker and lover and ever-present refuge for our souls.

Saying Goodbye

Josh, our worship pastor, came in my office the other day. As we chatted, I had the impression he was working up to something. Finally he said, "The time has come for us to move back to Minnesota to be closer to family." I took a deep breath, the kind I've needed on other occasions when I've received gut-churning news.

I love Josh and Kate. The thought of losing them initially felt like too much to bear. They have been a true blessing to our church. I really cannot imagine Platt Park Church without them. Through song and spirit, friendship, and serving, they have wiggled their way into our hearts, and we will never be the same.

In addition to my personal sense of loss, I also felt brief panic regarding our church's loss of such a dynamic pair of worship leaders. But God quickly reminded me that He really does provide for his church. This has been true to my experience every single time we have had great staff move on from our team. Josh and Kate will never be replaced, but God will provide. As in the past, we will probably step back, amazed by the person(s) He brings into our midst.

When God moves someone in leadership to a new place, it is for their good and also for the good of the church they are serving. It is ultimately for our good and His glory on both sides. This was certainly true for the church in Antioch. Paul and Barnabas were key leaders who helped establish the church in its newfound faith in Christ (Acts 11:19-26). Yet God very clearly called them away for a larger ministry (Acts 13:1-3). This would have been painful at first. But it also allowed new leadership to emerge in Antioch and the gospel mission to the Gentiles to rapidly expand (Acts 14:21-28). God's glory and His people's good went hand in hand.

Epilogue: When I first wrote this, I was not sure how the story would turn out. Today, I am thanking God for the gift of our new Pastor of Worship and Spiritual Formation, Charlie, his wife Liz, and baby Boaz. Charlie has brought a whole new thing to our faith community and I am grateful for the way God has worked in us all through this journey.

First Steps

Russell is a late walker. He is sixteen months old now, and he still walks on his knees. Here's the thing — he can walk. I see him do it, but he just moves so fast walking on his knees that I guess he thinks, *Why bother?* When the knee-walking works so well, the motivation to change just isn't very high.

I understand, Buddy. I'm late at a few things too. I'm late at learning that not every situation can be smoothed over, no matter how hard I try. I'm slow to accept that love and small resentments can coexist, and it doesn't mean the ship is sinking. I am sluggish to realize that almost everyone does what they do for a reason, and if I listen long enough, I may just come to understand why.

But you know what? Late is okay sometimes, and grace is for the late ones. First steps will come soon enough. In the meantime, from the first steps until the last steps, God's grace is sufficient for both of us.

"God opposes the proud but shows favor to the humble."

(James 4:6)

"But he said to me, 'My grace is sufficient for you, for my power is made perfect in weakness.' Therefore I will boast all the more gladly about my weaknesses, so that Christ's power may rest on me."

(2 Cor. 12:9)

An "I Used to Think" List

Gary Aronhalt recently spoke in our worship service and made a comment that everyone ought to have an "I used to think" list. I have pondered his idea ever since. We don't usually like to admit that we used to think or believe one way but have since changed our opinion. It means admitting we may have been wrong. Nevertheless, God gives grace to the humble (James 4:6). And the alternative means staying stuck and not progressing or growing as people. Am I proud of thinking the same things today that I thought when I was a preteen, teen, or young adult? Do I really imagine I have it all figured out today and will perceive myself, the world, and God the same when I am seventy? Most likely, many of my present suppositions will change over time, which is a mark of healthy personal and spiritual development.

So, I've been thinking. And here is my first draft of a list of things I used to think.

I used to think when people changed churches, they were flaky and just church-hopping. Now I think we have friends and faith communities for a reason, a season, or a lifetime. I used to think that, because I'm an ENTJ and logically minded, I wouldn't be a very sentimental mom. Now I see that parenting has opened up a part of my heart that I didn't think existed. I used to think if a woman made more money than her husband, they had a bad marriage and probably wouldn't make it. Now I realize people of quality are not threatened by equality. I used to think people could not be friends with their parents. Now I know I can. I used to think what a person believed was about all that mattered. Now I understand who we are, what we think, and how we behave are interconnected. I used to think God was stationary, like a rock. Now I believe God is on the move and active, like a world traveler. I used to think if I were rejected or publicly humiliated, I wouldn't survive. Now I know I can.

Perhaps for me there is a theme of growing a bit in the grace and freedom of my life in Christ (Gal. 5:1). All of us are called to grow in the grace and knowledge of Him (2 Pet. 3:18). I'm curious, what would you put on your list?

Lyla, GuGu, and Me

Lyla, our newly adopted two-year-old, affectionately calls her four-year-old brother Russell "GuGu," which means "big brother" in Mandarin. Lyla has gone through a huge adjustment, leaving her home country for a new one with a family that speaks a new language and looks different from the faces she is accustomed to seeing. One of the ways she's coped with this change is to attach to Russell. She adores him, looks up to him, follows him around, and takes cues from her GuGu.

Russell also has gone through a huge adjustment, from being the only kid in the house to immediately having a sister with whom he doesn't always want to share his toys, his time, or his parents. He is often tender and sweet towards Lyla, combing her hair and feeding her yogurt, but, sometimes, he reveals just how difficult this change has been for him. Today, he not-so-affectionately (but hilariously) said to Lyla, "I am not being your sister anymore!"

Transitions shape us. Sometimes they come to us abruptly or

violently, and, other times, we choose them joyfully, but they usually bring challenges. We will either become bitter or better through them. We find a way to embrace the change or find ourselves resisting, and possibly arguing about it, at every turn. Through changing seasons of life, our hope is to become more like Christ Jesus, the purpose for which God has predestined His people (Rom. 8:29).

During His greatest transition from being in heaven with the Father to living on earth through the incarnation, Jesus didn't resist but "being in very nature God, did not consider equality with God something to be used to his own advantage; rather, he made himself nothing by taking the very nature of a servant, being made in human likeness. And being found in appearance as a man, he humbled himself by becoming obedient to death—even death on a cross!" (Phil. 2:6–8). Jesus modeled extraordinary peacefulness and a lack of anxiety as he followed the Father's will in the changing seasons of His life.

After seminary, Tim and I moved to Iowa for Tim's job. Initially, I was eager for that transition and chose it, but once we arrived, I didn't embrace the changes easily. In my heart, I fought the changes that came wrapped in a move, a small town, a new church culture, and a new life. It was only through a combination of counseling, coaching, spiritual direction, and time that I found my way through that season.

In hindsight, I wish I had done some things differently. I regret my resistant attitude. Yet as hard as that experience was, I wouldn't remove it from my journey. In the end, it shaped me in positive ways. I'm grateful for the incredible guides I had along the way who compassionately listened, provided space, and challenged and guided me through that difficult terrain. God used them to remind me of spiritual truths, which transformed my thinking and living (Rom. 12:2).

Now, when I see others in transition, like Lyla and Russell, I remember the part these seasons play in our development, and I thank God for them.

The Sacred Practice
of Staying Put

I grew up in a church that really emphasized the importance of going. They spoke often of the directive to "go ye into all the world and make disciples" (Matt. 28:19). Every year, an elaborate missions festival highlighted all of the people from our church who had forsaken everything to follow Jesus by going to another part of the world to minister. I am grateful for the incredible people I know who have obeyed this call to go. They are doing important kingdom work, Jesus' own Great Commission work. However, sometimes the emphasis on this particular path of "leaving everything" to follow Him has diminished the worth of staying.

Tim and I moved eight times in the first twelve years of our marriage, but we have now lived in the same house for three years, a new record for us! I'm starting to see the value of staying in one spot. One beautiful by-product of staying is the opportunity to foster community. Kurt Vonnegut once said, "What should young people do with their lives today? Many things, obviously. But the most daring thing is to create stable communities in which the terrible disease of loneliness can be cured." Like tending a garden, fostering stable communities takes time, energy, love, and creativity. The community to which God calls me may be in another part of the world, or it may be right within my family, neighborhood, or office. For this season of our lives, God has called Tim and me to grow roots right here, in this home, with our two children and Platt Park Church. We are practicing taking relational risks, extending and receiving hospitality, engaging conflict in healthy ways, and enjoying humor and intimacy.

Another rich blessing of staying, ironically, has been the opportunity to explore how Christ's invitation to go is relevant for every follower of Christ. Going can mean living for Him right where we are, just as some disciples remained in Jerusalem while others went to the ends of the earth (Acts 1:8). Whether we travel far or stay close to what is familiar, often the hardest things to leave behind are the instincts that live and wage war inside of us. Relocation will never resolve our resentment, anger, jealousy, lust, fear of failure, competition, or need to prove our worthiness. We hold these internal attachments in the secret places of our hearts. They reside in our wishes, hopes, dreams, and fears rather than in our physical address. Often, these things go unnoticed and untended, but we need to take leave of them in order to fully follow Christ.

When Jesus tells us to go, He may have more than one possibility in mind! Jesus did His own leave-taking from His heavenly home to stay with us a while. He sacrificed Himself to bring salvation to us. Let's listen deeply for His particular invitation to us. Sometimes the most sacred thing you can do is stay put.

In the Weeds or Up
in the Treetops?

"Where there is no vision, the people perish: but he that keepeth the law, happy is he."

(Proverbs 29:18 KJV)

I studied leadership at Denver Seminary, and one thing most leadership gurus agree on is the importance of vision. This word "vision" can be intimidating. Sometimes it feels like it's about always being energetic and/or crystal clear on what you want and where you're going. But I think vision is really about caring, and caring deeply. If you have a vision for your family, you care deeply for them and want your kids to want to visit when they're thirty. If you have a vision for your marriage, you care deeply and want to grow old together even as you both change over the years. If you have a vision for your company, you care deeply and want to retain, develop, and engage your customers and staff. Vision is really about caring deeply.

I've been fascinated by survival stories. Why do some people survive and others perish in the same set of extreme circumstances? Perish is a strong word. It means to die, expire, rot, decay, wither, evaporate, vanish, disappear. Researchers have found that those who die simply lose hope. They give up caring and they perish.

Every day, you and I wake up and have the choice to be up in the treetop or down in the weeds. Much of life is lived in the weeds with things like filling up the car with gas, driving to work, figuring out what to eat, changing dirty diapers, paying bills, running the dishwasher again. But if we are only ever in the weeds and never up in the treetops, we begin to perish. We slowly wither on the inside. We might lose sight of how God has uniquely formed us for abundant life, joy, and participation in the Kingdom of God on earth.

I wonder what you can do today to get up in the treetops of your life. Something I've found helpful is to sit in my car before I go inside the office or my home, intentionally setting aside five minutes to take some deep breaths. I close my eyes, be silent, and listen to the voice of God, who has nothing but love and care for me. I believe true vision (deep caring) is born of God and is a gift He gives us as we create space in our lives to listen to Him. If this doesn't work for you, find something today that does.

What can you do today to step out of the weeds and foster a little "up in the treetops" time in your life?

Glory and Shame:
Lessons from My Sheepdog

Our sheepdog, Sam, just got shaved for the summer and looks totally different. When I brought him home, we told our friend, Curtis, who is living in our basement right now, that we got a new dog named Sam #2. I called Sam for what seemed like several minutes before he actually came out of his bathroom hiding spot to show off his new hairdo. He acts embarrassed when he gets shaved down. It's like he loses his glory and walks around ashamed for a while.

Glory and shame, naked and fig leaves, Sam fluffy and Sam shaved are all pictures of what God intended and what brokenness brings. Every day, I battle with shame and so do you. It's not a popular idea, but it's everywhere we look. Shame says you are not enough. Do more. Try harder. Be better. Get your act together. Shame shows up on the scale and in the mirror, in the kitchen, the bedroom, and the office.

Shame tells me I'm not a good parent, I'm unworthy of love, I'm not valuable.

Glory, on the other hand, is what God sees when He looks at you through Christ. He is actively working to transform us "into his image with ever-increasing glory" (2 Cor. 3:18). So, glory says, "You are my beloved. You have been bought at a price because I treasure you. My grace is sufficient for you. Rest, breathe, cease striving." Glory reminds me of my identity in Christ and of my destiny in heaven. "Therefore my heart is glad and my tongue rejoices; my body also will rest secure" (Ps. 16:9).

It is beautiful to see God's glory. May you have grace to trust His glory alive in you, and may others see His glory through you today.

Change and a Faith Community

I have always felt deep down to my toes that there is nothing like a faith community when it is working right. I witnessed this as a child, when my alcoholic father came to faith in Christ through the witness of a neighbor and the love of a local church. His life, and subsequently the entire trajectory of my family's life, changed dramatically. I have seen this life transformation happen over and over again, as Jesus and His church have partnered together.

Participating with God in transforming lives has always been the church's job, as we hear in Isaiah 58:6-7, when God defined true worship. "Is not this the kind of fasting I have chosen: to loose the chains of injustice and untie the cords of the yoke, to set the oppressed free and break every yoke? Is it not to share your food with the hungry and to provide the poor wanderer with shelter—when you see the naked, to clothe them, and not to turn away from your own flesh and blood?" Faith communities are working well when people care more about the things God cares about and less about the things He does not care about. God absolutely cares about recognizing and restoring beauty and wholeness in people.

Baptism is an acknowledgement that Jesus didn't just die for us a long time ago and then leave us to fend for ourselves. He invited us to follow Him, to die to our old selves and our former ways of living and being. He invites us to begin fresh and to participate with Him in extending this opportunity to others. Our immersion in the baptism waters is a picture of our dying with Christ in His death, and our emerging from the water represents our being raised to new life. A faith community that is working right holds this picture always before itself as a reminder of what God cares about, the healing and redemption of human lives.

This Sunday we are having baptisms, which I love because we gather together to witness and celebrate the stories of peoples' lives being changed by God. I cannot wait to celebrate baptism with the Platt Park church family this week.

PART 3

Compassion for Self

You do not have to be good.
You do not have to walk on your knees
For a hundred miles through the desert, repenting.
You only have to let the soft animal of your body
love what it loves.
Tell me about your despair, yours, and I will tell you mine.
Meanwhile the world goes on.
Meanwhile the sun and the clear pebbles of the rain
are moving across the landscapes,
over the prairies and the deep trees,
the mountains and the rivers.
Meanwhile the wild geese, high in the clean blue air,
are heading home again.
Whoever you are, no matter how lonely,
the world offers itself to your imagination,
calls to you like the wild geese, harsh and exciting—
over and over announcing your place
in the family of things.

—Mary Oliver, "Wild Geese"

Letter to My 2008 Self

Dear 2008 Susie,

Please take a deep breath and relax. This season of chaos in the church is revealing an unhealthy family system that has been in place for a long, long time. Try not to take all the turmoil so personally. The people who are leaving the church are not personally rejecting you, even when it feels that way. Keep looking into God's face. See His love for you. Hold on to Him, walk with integrity, love others, and take time to laugh with Tim and your home team of friends who love you no matter what your job or calling may be.

A day will come when you will feel total forgiveness and freedom from all this upheaval. You will feel this freedom in your heart and in your body. The weight will be lifted, like a balloon floating up in the air, and you will be free of anger. You will feel compassion toward the people whose decisions have hurt you so deeply. Time, hard work, God's healing, and counseling will give you a new perspective on all of this. It's going to be okay.

So, hold your head up and remember God is still on the throne. Even though it's brutal right now, this hardship is forming you in a thousand positive little ways.

With love and grace and tears of gladness,
Your 2013 Susie

I wanted to share this because all suffering at the time seems overwhelming and final, but in my experience, God has proven to be the redeemer that Scripture says He is, taking the broken rubble to make something beautiful. I hope this truth encourages those who are facing painful experiences and, perhaps, relational conflict or disappointment right now. I have heard people use the word "brutiful" to describe the combination of brutal plus beautiful in life. May you step into your struggles with God and move towards your brutiful life today.

Rate Me

Every time I get an Amazon delivery, I also receive a text message asking me to "rate my experience." The text reads, "Your package with Pampers Baby Dry Diapers has been delivered by the carrier. Rate it right here at amazon.com/box." Really? Rate my experience? Let's see, hmmm. I ordered the diapers, and then they arrived. Great job, everyone.

We live in a world that constantly prompts us to judge. Rate your experience, size up your competition, weigh her beauty, gauge his sincerity. Look. Evaluate. Assess. Judge. These activities have a legitimate place in our lives. We weigh options for their risks and benefits (Luke 14:28). We attempt to discern right from wrong (1 Cor. 11:31–32). We listen for truth and goodness in an effort to protect ourselves from deception (Eph. 5:1–6). We teach our children discernment (Eph. 6:4).

But judging can become a habit. And once judgment becomes habit, I am prone to being critical. I don't want to be known for a critical spirit, which Christ so often condemned (Matt. 7:1-2). I want to be about welcome, hospitality, and spiritual formation. I want to be focused on others and active service. I want to develop a disposition that says, "This is enough. You are enough. I am enough. Relax and rest," rather than a personality that is always rating myself and others and concluding, "More, better, faster, higher. You could really do better next time."

This vision of myself is not yet reality. I'm a driver. I run fast and hard, and I seek continual improvement. I need God's words in my ear every moment reminding me, as He reminded Jesus, "You are my beloved, precious in my eyes." It is counter-cultural to allow myself, my circumstances, and others to be enough, to cease striving and rest in gratitude and joy. I want to live each day with less of an Amazon "rate me" philosophy and more of a Scriptural conviction: Christ in me, "the hope of glory." (Col. 1:27)

Gentle Reminders to Myself

My life is a little crazy these days. Besides co-leading a church with Tim, my family and I are moving into the church parsonage in January. I run a small side business we own, we are adopting a child, I am mom to a boy who is straddling the line between baby and toddler, and it's almost Christmas. So, I've decided to create a little list of instructions for myself to follow this month, just so I can be present and connected to God through Advent and keep everything in perspective when life is full.

Gentle reminders for surviving the holidays:

1. Go to your small group and tell everyone how you're really doing, even if you sound stupid, or cry, or think they think you're something other than fine.

2. Avoid Pinterest for vague dreaming that only leaves you feeling inadequate.

3. Use Pinterest only if you will actually implement a brilliant idea like removing some foul mildew smell in your towels. (http://pinterest.com/pin/260153315946229335/)

4. End the phone call before walking into the house after work.

5. Leave the phone on the counter when playing with Russell in his room. Sit on the floor with him, and whatever you do, do not try to multitask because you'll be frustrated, both he and the task will suffer, and you might miss something special.

6. Walk the dog with Tim and Russell every morning. Wear warm clothes so that you can actually enjoy it.

7. Let yourself cry when you see the kids in your neighborhood walking into school, imagining Russell being that big and independent someday.

8. Call Mom.

9. Don't start thinking it's a good idea to bake a lot right now when you read that foodie blog.

10. When crazy kicks in, take a deep breath, put your feet flat on the floor, and deeply breathe in the presence of God, here and now.

11. Accept that there are only twenty-four hours in this day, relinquish the list, and trust that you are right where you are supposed to be. Then say your prayers, kiss Tim, and let the bed hold you up before falling asleep.

What gentle reminders are you giving yourself these days? Are there ways you've neglected to take care of yourself? What can you do to change that?

So Proud of You

On our last full day together as a team in Guatemala, we sat around a long dining room table nestled in a cozy casita in the middle of the rain forest, sharing our appreciation for each team member. Each person took a turn at being in the "hot seat" and was only allowed to say "thank you" as the others shared what they appreciated about them during our week of serving and traveling together. At times, the awkwardness was almost palpable as those who preferred to stay in the background were pushed to the spotlight for a moment. But we patiently persisted in sharing our words of love with one another.

One of our team members, ten-year-old Henry, is a wonderful mix of all-boy and old-soul. He sat smiling and nodding, eagerly soaking up all our praise of his truly special self. I will carry what happened next with me for the rest of my life. After all the other team members shared, his dad leaned across the table and looked his son in the eyes. "Henry, as your dad, you know I'm hard on you. I really ride you and stay on top of you. But, Henry, I want you to know I could not be more proud of you. God has given us an amazing gift in having you as our son, and I couldn't be more proud to be your dad." On hearing these words, Henry lowered his face, covered it with his hands, and started crying. I cried too, along with most of the rest of our team. Under the hot, humid canopy of the Guatemalan jungle that night, one dad took the time to share the words every child (and adult) needs to hear.

Henry's dad gave us an unforgettable picture of pure, direct, affirming, and honest love. Our whole group was moved because we recognized how rare, yet how essential, such exchanges are.

May we all take the instruction of the apostle Paul and the example of Henry's dad and put our words into action to encourage those we love today. "Therefore encourage one another and build each other up." (1 Thess. 5:11)

Shame Fest

Last week over dinner, Tim said, "Susie, I think you are a great mom, but I am kind of sick of the road block I hit when I try to express that to you. So, I'm not going to try to tell you that you're a great mom anymore. You have such a strong resistance in your mind that you just cannot receive my words."

I didn't really like being called out on my shame fest. I know how frustrating it is to offer encouragement to someone, only to be met with a wall of resistance because the other person just cannot accept the compliment. I was a little shocked that my shame had reached this level in my life and was creating a rift between Tim and me.

I had to admit Tim's observation was true. All my recent traveling has left me feeling like a bad mom. The weight of that self-doubt and self-criticism is unbearable. I don't know any parents who don't at least occasionally question whether they're doing a good job. Parenting is a big task, and there is no manual. Still, I don't want to live in shame or allow it to shape my sense of worth and purpose. I want God to shape my life. I want my roles as mother, wife, and pastor to be grounded in God's love, grace, and wisdom.

So I told Tim I'd make him a deal. If he'd agree to keep offering encouragement and affirmation, I'd agree to change my response, even if it were forced and fake at first. I told him that if he complimented or encouraged me about my parenting, I would immediately drop onto one knee and say, "Yes!" like a quarterback scoring in the end zone. I figured dramatic measures are called for in drastic circumstances. The truth is I am a good parent. Not always, and not perfectly, but I'm doing my best, and God offers me grace for the rest. The same is true for you.

The truest thing about you is not what you say about yourself in your head. The truest thing about you is what God says about you. And He says you are deeply loved. The Bible says that perfect love casts out fear. God invites us to live in His perfect love. This love has the power to transform us from the inside out, if we'll only receive and abide in it.

Wherever your shame resides, I invite you to join me on a counter-mission to try to re-wire and exchange your self-critical thoughts for God's thoughts. The next time someone offers you kind words about an area of your life where you feel discouraged and unworthy, please do an end-zone dance for me, to God's glory.

"And we all, who with unveiled faces contemplate the Lord's glory, are being transformed into his image with ever-increasing glory, which comes from the Lord, who is the Spirit."

(2 Cor. 3:18)

That One Small Word

I just had coffee with someone I haven't seen in a long time and, while we were talking, he brought up a situation in my life that still feels broken, despite superficial "fine-ness" with the people involved and enormous efforts at repair. I'm not sure why I felt the need to hide, but I did my best to poker-face my way through the conversation, pushing the sadness away from my eyes, concealing the pain that still remains.

As I left the coffee shop, I felt sad and a little ashamed. Before returning to the office, I walked around the neighborhood to pray, clear my head, and re-center myself. Instead, my feelings only intensified. Instead of finding peace, I dove headlong into worry, shame, and fears. In rehearsing my anxieties, I started to feel worse and worse. I wanted to "walk it off," but when "it" is on the inside, walking doesn't always work. Because I'm committed to living in freedom, honesty, forgiveness, gratitude, and grace, it's hard for me to accept a situation or relationship's brokenness, especially after doing everything in my power to reconcile, without success.

So, what do you do when there is a hurt that might never fully heal? What do you do when you've done all you know to do and the situation still feels a little broken? When you're a fixer, and you just can't fix it? When there are no songs on your shuffle playlist that will comfort the prick inside? When you are a pastor and you need to be pastored? When you need to be guided to a place that you cannot get to on your own?

I usually call my counselor or spiritual director, or I journal, or I talk to one of my small circle of trusted "home team" friends. Today, I did all of that. From the collective wisdom these encounters provided, one truth strikes me most: I need acceptance. I need to accept God's grace for the past. I need to accept what cannot be changed (à la Serenity prayer). I need to accept that the past is the past. That one *little word* — accept — might make the difference between my moving forward and my staying stuck.

May you too work to change what can be changed, and may you accept what needs accepting in your life today.

Hosting Dinner with
No Countertops

When Tim and I were first married, I really rolled out the red carpet when hosting friends for dinner or out-of-town company for the weekend. I love entertaining, so making our house look like Pottery Barn (on a Target budget) was fun for me. One of our early-married fights was about me wanting to go all out for guests and Tim wanting to serve my parents pizza and beer on paper plates. Now, after eleven years of being married, I have to say this is one area that has really changed for me. I still enjoy hosting beautiful dinners, but I have also come to appreciate time with people more than what we're eating or how it all looks.

So, this morning, I invited the neighbors for dinner. They are coming over at five o'clock and our house is a total (not joking) construction zone. I'm preparing meals on the plywood countertop, there is an uninstalled dishwasher in the middle of the kitchen, and all the windows are completely bare. But, we have a table and we have chairs and it will be a memory when I offer them a glass of wine in one of Russell's sippy cups because I still can't find the box with the wine glasses in it. If I wait until everything is perfect, I probably won't be hosting for a while because this house needs a lot of updating. So, I've decided to just move forward with having people over in the midst of our mess and not worry about it. Relationships, faith, and gratitude in the middle of a construction zone describe my life today.

It seems there are two ways to live. One says, "I will be grateful when [fill in the blank]," and the other says, "I will be grateful now." You can say, "I will be grateful when my house is done, or when I get that job, or find the right girl." Or you can say, "I will be grateful now." You choose.

Psalm 118:26 NKJV says, "*This* is the day that the Lord has made; We will rejoice and be glad in it" (emphasis mine). It does not say tomorrow is the day God has made, or yesterday but rather "this is the day."

What can you be grateful for today?

Adopting Lyla
Part 3

We were sitting in a required parent training for adoption a couple years ago when the facilitator started explaining that there is a "primal wound" that occurs when a birth mother and a child are separated shortly after birth. She was teaching from a well-known resource by Nancy Verrier, called *The Primal Wound: Understanding the Adopted Child*. The focus of both the book and the class was the effects of adoption on the adopted. The big idea is that all adoptees, even those adopted at birth, experience a bond break that creates a deep emotional wound and that a loving set of adoptive parents can help to heal the wound.

One woman in our class listened to all the unique challenges of bonding and attaching inherent in adoption and then finally blurted out, "This is so depressing! I'm not even sure I want to adopt anymore!"

Tim and I listened, learned, were sobered by the realizations, but didn't feel any less drawn to adopt. For us, it felt empowering to know the information. It felt honest to acknowledge and embrace the research.

Just like there is a romance to things past that may have been difficult at the time, there can be a romance to adoption. Romantic ideas play a role in initially drawing us, inspiring us toward a beautiful vision of what could be. But it's a limited view. It's only a small part of the true story. Real love — the tough, weathered, true kind — doesn't remain starry-eyed forever. Authentic love is sometimes boring, sometimes brutal, sometimes messy and scary and roll-up-your-sleeves, push-on, one-foot-forward hard work. It bears the burdens of others (Gal. 6:2), speaks the truth in love (Eph. 4:15), and "covers over a multitude of sins" (1 Pet. 4:8). Romance comes and goes. Sustaining love, on the other hand, embraces the truth, lives informed, and rides the seasons of winter, spring, summer, and fall. It never fails (1 Cor. 13:8).

I want to be the kind of person who moves beyond romance to give and receive sustaining love. I want to offer this kind of love to my people, to my kids, to Tim, and to our home team. I want more than pseudo-community that's all about conflict-avoidance. I want the real deal. I want to foster authentic community that is born when we risk vulnerability and are willing to enter the tunnel of chaos to find one another as we truly are.

Embracing "the primal wound" of adoption is just a picture to me of embracing people for who they really are (not who I want to make them be) and not minimizing the pain of our unique human experiences, whatever they may be. This takes humility, vulnerability, patience, and time. It's relevant in all my relationships. We all have different pains and wounds, and we all have the chance to offer one another healing.

The Lowest RSVP Rate
in the Nation

Colorado has the lowest RSVP rate in the nation. We are a state of people who like to keep our options open. We don't want to be too nailed down. We like our freedom. Open options, extreme flexibility, and self-determination are not bad values. They allow us to express our God-given preferences and explore the wide world which has been entrusted to us, at least partially, for our enjoyment. They allow space for the spontaneity often conducive to creativity.

But living in a "low RSVP rate" setting has some limitations. We cannot build a foundation of caring communities if we are primarily concerned with keeping our options open, remaining flexible, and determining our own destinies. Caring communities require personal investment. Investment consists of some level of risk in the areas of depth and intimacy, as well as some willingness to defer to the preferences of others, and even to mutually agreed upon boundaries. This was certainly the example set by the early church. In addition to regularly meeting for worship and learning from the apostles, they "sold property and possessions to give to anyone who had need. Every day they continued to meet together in the temple courts. They broke bread in their homes and ate together with glad and sincere hearts, praising God" (Acts 2:45-47).

Think of such communities as those shared in Olympic team sports such as relay, basketball, or soccer. For the sake of a shared victory, the players invest themselves in a long preparation process. They spend concentrated time together, learning each other's strengths and weaknesses. They accept correction and counsel from each other and from their coach. They practice together, determining the best ways to honor the rules of the game while also highlighting each member's unique contribution. Players commit to each other, to their coach, to the game, and to their country, united by a common goal.

Whether in an Olympic team setting or a church family, depth and intimacy require a commitment to "showing up" and actively engaging that directly opposes the culture's value of keeping options open. God tells us to "consider how we may spur one another on toward love and good deeds, not giving up meeting together, as some are in the habit of doing, but encouraging one another" (Heb. 10:24-25). How do you see yourself buying into Colorado's "low RSVP rate?" How has this benefited and/or limited you and those around you? How has it impacted your ability to form authentic relationships?

Why I Love Child Dedication

As a Pastor, Mother's Day makes me a little nervous every year. I am always aware that it may be a painful day, a joyful day, a salt-in-the-wound day, or a sacred day, depending on your experience. It is also a beautiful opportunity to acknowledge that, anytime someone chooses to nurture and care for another human being, they are "mothering" in the best definition of that word.

I'm not sure if it's always been the case throughout the history of parenting, but I know that the parents I speak with today, myself included, regularly feel some shame in their job as parents. If you pull a busy parent aside and say, "You're doing a great job," don't be surprised if they break into tears. Maybe the high expectations of our culture prevent us from feeling we can measure up. Maybe every parent just has days when they want to resign from the job and then feels guilty for wanting to. Or maybe it's because little kids are just so unrelenting in their needs.

So, when parents stand up and dedicate themselves and their children to God, it is a declaration of dependence. It is the best possible cry for help. It is a full-on, complete acknowledgement that we cannot do this job alone. We need God, we need our friends and family, and we need our church community. There aren't many places where you can stand and say "I need a ton of help here" and then make a celebration and ceremony out of how totally awesome that is to admit to the world.

Thank you in advance to all the families who will share heartfelt letters to their children with us in church tomorrow. Thank you for modeling dependence and your need for help. Thank you for modeling courage and strength for all of us. Thank you for being a part of our church.

You don't need one more person needing you right now, but the truth is we need you too. Our church needs you. We don't need you to do anything extra. We just need you to be in our lives because what you are doing in raising children is important. When we see your sacrifice, we remember why Jesus said, "Let the little children come to me." We are reminded that God is found in serving the littlest and least of these. You're doing a great job.

About Being Unplugged

One of the best parts about marrying into the Grade family is the annual "Up North" tradition. It's that week every summer of Tim's entire life (and mine, after we married) when we hit the lake in northern Wisconsin. We exchange our 4G network for a spotty connection and trade in our busy schedules for lazy days. Leaving all work clothes at home, we rely mainly on swimsuits, flip-flops, and shorts and T-shirts. For hours, we stare at the lake rather than our screens, and we get loads of time with some of the people we love most. But in our attempt to unplug from all the movement that is our daily lives, we usually find ourselves antsy for activity and hot with cabin fever by Day 3.

This past week, we've been up north and I'm reminded once again that there is just something good about non-productivity and not striving. There is something strong birthed by quiet and by letting the beauty of nature seep past the clamor within.

Most days this week during Russell's nap, I sat on the boat or on the dock staring up at those tall trees surrounding the lake. I watched and reveled and soaked in all the beauty of the wind rustling in the pines, the deer wandering by, and the water lapping up against the shore. I found my heart singing for no particular reason beyond that I am here and God is here and we are here together.

I wish for you a moment, or many moments, like this in your summer. May we all better learn to trust that when God tells us to rest, He really does mean it. And He has non-flashy, undetectable, life-giving gifts waiting for us there.

Consuming Fire

Recently, after some time in silence and prayer with my spiritual director, an image of God's Spirit as holy fire pervaded my mind. I desire the fire of God's Spirit to purify my life. Fire understandably sounds scary to us. We don't want to be burned. But as I reflected on this image of God, I was drawn to the fire and inspired by all the good in it.

God's Spirit is like a fire that consumes everything that isn't love in my life: my ego, my agenda, my competitiveness, my fear, my hoarding mentality. In the presence of God's Holy Spirit, all of that is burned away. What remains is this simple truth: God is love and I am in God, so I am loved. This is the gold that is purified when all else burns away. When I quiet myself to sit and receive His love like a child, I become aware of all the other things I was seeking and propping up for His approval and the approval of others. In the stillness, it all gets stripped away, and the truest things about God and about me emerge. These pure truths are all I ever want and all I ever need.

For several years now, I have embraced the practice of meeting with a Christian spiritual director. Spiritual direction is simply the practice of being with someone as you attempt to deepen your relationship with God. My spiritual director usually guides us to begin our time together in silence. When I leave spiritual direction, I leave the silence. Almost immediately, as I drive down Santa Fe Boulevard, a host of little ambitions, distractions, and agendas reemerge in my mind and heart. Silence leads me into the presence of Holy God, Consuming Fire. I need that daily practice so that my life may be constantly distilled and purified.

Get a Cue

Yesterday at church I got to hug an expectant mom about to have her first baby. She told me that she is physically ready, but she's been very sad about the "married with no children" season of life coming to an end.

I can relate. Tim and I were married for ten years before Russell was born. I remember being eight months pregnant and so eager to meet our little sprout, but simultaneously so sad to say goodbye to that decade of just the two of us. I was grieving the end of an era that would never come again, saying goodbye to a part of my life that had been full of sweetness and difficulty and change and growth.

Now we are in this new stage called "raising young children." When Russell goes to kindergarten, I'm sure I'll grieve the loss of this stage too. All too soon, I'm told, he will graduate from high school and go off into the world, which is both a loss and a joy I cannot even imagine right now.

Talking with my pregnant friend got me thinking about how completely not in-the-moment I tend to live. I'm almost always thinking about what is gone or what is next. I imagine the future, thinking about tonight or tomorrow, next week or next year, or in the case of Russell's graduation sixteen years from now!

Recently, Tim's mom came and stayed with us for two weeks. She often sang a song to Russell, called "Jesus' Love is Sweet." We've kept singing it since she left, and I've been making it my practice to use that little jingle as a personal cue to pause and be in the moment. As we sing it countless times each day, I slow myself, center myself, and deeply breathe in the presence and love of God and the sweetness of this season. Even if there are fish crackers all over the car and smushed bananas on my new couch!

Maybe you can find a cue that's helpful to you when you find yourself pulled into the past or catapulted into the future. Whatever life stage you find yourself in, whether good or bad, heartbreaking or exhilarating, you can be sure that it will not last. So be present to it, knowing that our Lord holds our past, present, and future securely, and His love endures forever. And nothing can separate from that love (Rom. 8:35–39). Remember Paul's words: "Do not be anxious about anything, but in every situation, by prayer and petition, with thanksgiving, present your requests to God." (Phil. 4:6)

Identify the ways that you get caught up in the past or focus too much on the future. What are the things that trigger these thought patterns? What are some ways you can practice being present in your day-to-day life? What thoughts or habits do you need to lay aside?

Baby, Don't Struggle

When our one-year-old son, Russell, doesn't want to have his diaper changed, or his clothes put on, or get in his car seat, he can put up quite a struggle for a twenty-some pounder. Gabby, our au pair, will often say in her Chinese accent, "Baby, don't struggle." When I hear her, I wonder if God ever says something like that to me. When Russell struggles against something that is so obviously good for him, I wish I could communicate in a way he could understand. "Baby, this seatbelt will keep you safe," I might say, and he would smile and calmly settle back against the seat. I suppose he'll learn as he grows.

I wonder if, when I struggle, God longs to communicate His heart to me in the same way. "Baby," He might say, "don't struggle with fear. I've got the whole world in my hands. Don't concern yourself with what others think. The only one who matters has already weighed in and is absolutely crazy about you. Baby, don't struggle to prove yourself right or influential or put-together or justified. If I am for you, then who can be against you?" And I would lean back against His promises and rest. I suppose I'll have to learn as I grow too.

Off to Israel

I'm heading to Israel this week for a tour of the Holy Land with more than thirty other pastors. I'm absolutely delighted to be going and simultaneously dreading being away from Russell for a full nine days. I know, it's only nine days, but I'm going to miss that little man! I remember my childhood pastor, Stuart Briscoe, telling stories about missionaries back in the day who packed their belongings in a coffin and sang the old hymn, "I'll See You Someday in Heaven," as they kissed their loved ones forever goodbye at the boat dock and headed to the mission field. It reflected Jesus' teaching about the sacrificial nature of following Him. He said, "If anyone comes to me and does not hate father and mother, wife and children, brothers and sisters—yes, even their own life—such a person cannot be my disciple. And whoever does not carry their cross and follow me cannot be my disciple." (Luke 14:26–27)

I wonder if there is any modern-day equivalent of such total abandonment to God and calling? Leaving family, friends, comfort, home, and land to follow God's calling when there was no Internet and only a slow boat in one direction seems to me now to be so single-minded, so final, so fully abandoned. Where are today's examples, in the United States, of people who are "abandoning all" in surrender to God's call on their lives? Maybe I'm just being nostalgic about the old-school missionary stories, but I wonder sometimes if we haven't lost something.

What do you think? Do you have any present-day stories of people who have sacrificed deeply to follow their understanding of Jesus' mission for them?

As I say goodbye to my sweet Russell for the next nine days, I remember and honor others who have gone before me and modeled gracious openhandedness with the people and possessions dearest to them.

I Miss It

We had dinner last week with Charlie, our new pastor of worship and spiritual formation, and his wife, Liz. On our way out the door, Russell, our three-year old, picked up a craft he had made in preschool and said, "I give Charlie?" We said, "Sure, you can give that to Charlie." Upon our arrival, Russell handed his craft to Charlie and Liz as a little gift. They oohed and aahed and asked Russell if he had made it.

As we were getting ready to leave, Russell picked up that same craft and started walking out the door with it. I said, "Russell, I thought you gave that to Charlie and Liz."

He frowned and said, "I miss it."

Aren't material attachments strange? That craft is one among fifty laying around our house. We throw some away every day to control the clutter. But for some reason, Russell had a hard time parting with the craft he had given to Charlie and Liz. I can relate to Russell's little dilemma. I want to be generous, but I also want stuff. I want to give, but I also want to keep. I want to live open-handedly, but I find myself clutching tightly. We forget that everything we have is a gift from God (1 Cor. 4:7; James 1:17).

Yesterday, we received a few coins in an offering envelope at church with these words written inside, "I gave what I had. May not be much at all, but hopefully it will help. God bless." It was similar to a small offering Jesus praised in his day (Mark 12:42–44). This beautiful offering reminds me of the spiritual power released in and through us when we give. Jesus said, "It is more blessed to give than to receive" (Acts 20:35). Then, he modeled this through His ordinary interactions and astonishing miracles. May we follow in the steps of the One who gave freely and fully.

When People Leave

On a regular basis, people come to our church, and, on a regular basis people also leave. For all sorts of reasons, they leave. This is a painful part of being a pastor. I'm very grateful that more people are coming than going these days, but every person who leaves is a loss, not just to the church in an abstract way, but to me personally and to our staff. As a pastor, I hold people in my heart in a deep way. I carry their stories with me. It's not a matter of if people will leave our church, but rather a matter of when. Each goodbye is painful, sometimes heart-wrenching.

When we decided to adopt a child from China, we imagined a child who was all alone, perhaps in a crib, with little attention or love. After we were "matched" with Lyla, we discovered quite a different story! Lyla was in a home with the most fabulous and loving foster family. Hulu, her foster mom, began video chatting with me daily so Lyla could get to know her new mom, even months before we met. We sent videos back and forth each day, and I sang to Lyla and read her stories. Hulu played those videos for Lyla when we were still thousands of miles apart. When we finally met face-to-face, Lyla had been prepared in countless ways to be family.

The journey of a foster family is one of loving deeply and fully, and then letting go. Letting go is the final act of love. It is a picture of sacrificial love that is vulnerable, beautiful, and impossible to fully honor. We are blessed that Hulu and her family gave Lyla (and us) that gift. They will always love her in their hearts, but they held her loosely in their hands. They knew one day Lyla would no longer be in their home, though she will always be in their hearts. This is the excruciating work of love. Someday, Lyla and I will go visit Hulu again in China, once again into her doors.

I am now having to cope with the dynamic of loving and losing that is inherent to ministry. Sometimes, as a church, we are an adoptive family, and other times we are a foster family. We don't always know which one we will be when someone walks through our doors. But, either way, our job is the same — to love people. Love people like family. Love people deeply, fully, and fearlessly. If the possibility of someone leaving tomorrow keeps me from loving them fully today, then fear wins. And Scripture says, "There is no fear in love. But perfect love drives out fear" (1 John 4:18).

Some will leave because their time with us was only for a reason or a season. I want to be like Hulu in these moments of departure. I will cry and grieve. I may even wish things were different. At the same time I will remember this is what we are made to do. We are made to love, and sometimes loving means letting go.

Our weekly benediction says, "May the peace of the Lord Christ go with you, wherever He may send you. May He guide you through the wilderness, protect you through the storm. May He bring you home rejoicing at the wonders He has shown you. May He bring you home rejoicing once again into our doors."

The door of my heart remains open toward the person who leaves, so that they can go where God leads them with my love and blessing. If they ever need this family again, we are here. We are always here. We will love you when you come, and we will love you as you go. We will love you when you fall away and flake out. If you choose to return, we will love you then as well. After all, our job is to love one another as we have been loved by God.

Hulu and I still regularly exchange photos. She sends Lyla the most amazing gifts. I am forever grateful that Lyla has so many people all around the world who love her so deeply. So, for those of you who have left our flock, and for those of you who may, please know that you will always have a special place in my heart. I'm honored to be one of the pastors who has played a small part in your journey.